Diwali is a wonderful time of year
that reminds us when good deeds were victorious.
It's a day filled with special things,
and a time to celebrate our blessings.

It's a season that fills our hearts and homes
with gentle warmth and light
that brings each and every one of us
plenty of delight.

We make beautiful rangoli on the ground
to make our homes welcoming,
for friends and family will come visit us
and bring good luck and season's greetings.

We light up beautiful oil lamps.

Oh, there are so many kinds!

The soft warm glow that twinkles

makes us smile big smiles.

Everyone gets all dressed up

in brand new Indian clothes.

It's all very colorful and stunning,

and the fun is only beginning.

A visit to the temple is always a delight

it's something to look forward to.

There are amazing temples to choose from

it's hard to choose which ones to go to.

9

We perform puja for Ganesha and Lakshmi
and thank them for keeping us well.
New efforts are begun today
with their blessings as we ring the bell.

No Diwali is complete
without super yummy sweets.
With many to choose from,
tasty foods fill up our tum-tums!

Our homes are filled with family and friends
who are glad to visit each other
to share and join the celebrations
and make new memories together.

Getting together with cousins
and neighbors and friends to play...
and lighting up all the fireworks
are the best parts of the day!

Colorful fireworks burst in the night sky.

What a spectacular sight to see!

The glittering sky with crackling booms

makes it thrilling for you and me.

The day is marked by the kind of sharing
that fills our hearts, tummies and pockets.
Even grown-ups get into the fiery fun
of spinners, sparklers and rockets.

Grandma tells us the story of Diwali

of Rama and Sita's life

And of how good overcame the bad

the way we should live and strive

Diwali is always very special

packed with joyful memories.

It's all about good times with friends and family.

Wish you a very happy Diwali!